14 Days

Oceanography

One of the newest oceanographic research vessels afloat is the U.S. Navy's Hayes. Her twin hulls provide greater stability at sea and increased laboratory space below.

Oceanography

BY JEROME WILLIAMS

◄─A FIRST BOOK─►

Franklin Watts, Inc. / New York / 1972

For Pam and Bobby

Acknowledgments / Cover design by Seymour
Schlatner. U.S. Navy: Frontis, pp. viii, 58, 60, 62, 64,
67. Vantage Art, Inc.: pp. 3, 4, 7, 9, 12, 15, 24, 26, 27,
29, 32, 36, 41, 43, 45, 46, 49, 50, 52, 56, 57. Raytheon
Company: 4. Woods Hole Oceanographic Institution:
11. American Museum of Natural History: 17.
Westinghouse Underseas Division: 21, 22. Plessey
Electronics: 47. NASA: 65.

Library of Congress Cataloging in Publication Data

Williams, Jerome, 1926-
    Oceanography.

    (A First book)
    SUMMARY: Introduces the various aspects of
oceanography, the scientific study of the oceans and
marine animals and plants.
    1. Oceanography–Juvenile literature. [1. Ocean-
ography] I. Title.
PZ10.W6570c   551.4′6   72-2336
ISBN 0-531-00775-8

Contents

Oceanography

LIGHT FADES OUT   THERMOCLINE   CONTINENTAL SHELF 350—500 FT.

SCATTERING LAYER

2000 FT.

BATHYSPHERE
(WM. BEEBE)
3028 FT.

WHALE TO 3000 FT.

BENTHOSCOPE
(OTIS BARTON)
4500 FT.

1 MILE

10,000 FT.
2.17 TONS/IN^2
2 MILES

MEAN SEA DEPTH
12,447 FT.

GREAT OCEANIC BASINS
12,000—16,000 FT.

FNRS—3
13.287 FT.

3 MILES

20,000FT.
4.34 TONS/IN^2

4 MILES

DEEP SEA CAMERA

5 MILES

30,000 FT.
6.36 TONS/IN^2

6 MILES

BATHYSCAPH TRIESTE
CHALLENGER DEEP
35,800 FT.

8.00 TONS/IN^2

An Introduction to
Oceanography and Oceanographers

Since man first made his home by the water, he has profited from the sea. It has protected him from his enemies and carried his commerce. It has supplied him with food and provided a convenient dumping ground for his waste. As his knowledge of the oceans increased, man found more ways to use the sea and to profit from it. Today we know something about waves and currents so that our ships can travel more safely, but still some run aground or sink. We know of the minerals present on the ocean bottom, but we do not know in what quantities they exist nor exactly where they are located. We know of the fish and the chemical substances present in the ocean, but in both cases we do not yet know how to exploit these resources to the maximum. We know that the ocean affects, and even controls, our weather, but we do not know exactly how and to what extent.

These problems and many more besides are the concern of *oceanography*, the science of the sea. It is performed by men and women who specialize in the marine application of such basic sciences as geology, biology, chemistry, and physics. As might be expected, these people are called geological oceanographers, biological oceanographers, chemical oceanographers, and physical oceanographers, and we shall examine some of their activities in the following pages.

It is difficult to pinpoint the exact beginning of oceanography as a science. Some say that Curtius Rufus, a Roman who lived about 300 B.C. and who succeeded in relating the cause of the tides to the moon, was the first oceanographer. Others reserve this distinction for Matthew Fontaine Maury, an American naval officer, who pub-

Composite sketch shows various milestones in oceanographic research as well as underwater topography. Pressure per square inch for successive depths is given at left.

lished the initial textbook on physical oceanography in 1855. Maury's book, *The Physical Geography of the Sea*, was largely devoted to describing the causes of the Gulf Stream. Although his theories have greatly been disproved, Maury was nevertheless the first modern-day scientist to conduct a serious study of the sea; and for his efforts he is remembered as the "Pathfinder of the Seas."

The Immensity of the Ocean

The ocean is wet, salty, and huge. It is so immense that it covers about 70 percent of the earth's surface. Only about three-tenths of our globe is covered with land.

The large amount of water compared to the small amount of land on the earth's surface may be emphasized by imagining all of the continents jammed together in one corner of the globe. In actuality, of course, the continents are not bunched together like this, but are spread out over the entire earth's surface. However, most geological oceanographers think that a long time ago in the earth's history all of the continents were once grouped closely together in much this manner.

The oceans are thousands of miles wide, and yet the average oceanic depth is only two or three miles. The world ocean is really a very thin layer of water covering most of the surface of the planet earth. Its measurements could be compared to a page of this book. The ratio of the thickness of this book page to its width is just about the same as the ratio of the ocean's average depth to its breadth.

Situated in the ocean are the seven continents, which are arranged in a very unusual manner. Most of them are located in the Northern Hemisphere with only a few in the Southern. Usually if there is a land mass in one part of the world, directly opposite it on the globe there is a water mass. The most obvious example of this is the Arctic Ocean which covers the area around the North Pole, as contrasted with the Antarctic continent which covers the area around the South Pole.

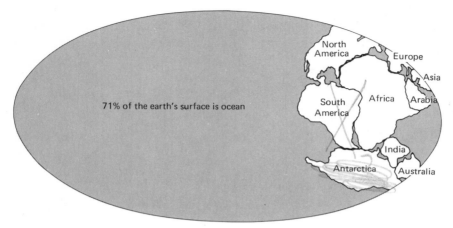

North
America
Europe
Asia
Africa
Arabia
South
America
71% of the earth's surface is ocean
India
Antarctica
Australia

If all the continents were crammed into one corner of the earth like this, the vast extent of the world ocean could easily be seen.

From Continental Shelf to Ocean Basin — Mapping the Ocean Floor

If a tourist were to board a ship and travel across the ocean, measuring the water depth as he went, he would find that depth would remain very much the same for the first portion of his voyage. Later on he would note a very sudden increase in depth as the ship steamed farther out to sea. Still farther out, he would find large areas where again the depth was relatively constant but, of course, much deeper.

This first portion of the ocean bottom, next to the continents, where the bottom is relatively level, is called the *continental shelf.* The region of the ocean bottom where the depth increases very rapidly away from the continental land masses is called the *continental slope.* The final, greater depths which are relatively constant for large areas of the ocean bottom are called the *ocean basins.*

Oceanographers know these features exist because much effort

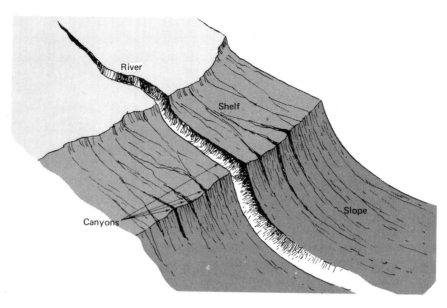

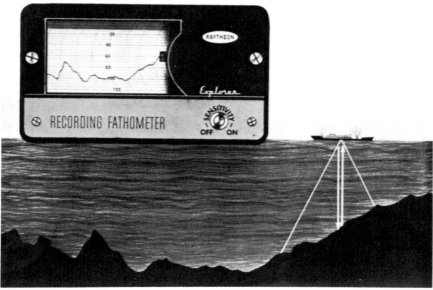

has been spent on mapping the ocean bottom. In order to make such maps, the depth of the ocean must be known in many places. In former times, seamen made depth determinations called *soundings* by means of a lead line. This was simply a long piece of rope, marked off in fathoms (six-foot intervals) and having a lead weight at one end. The depth was measured by dropping the weight into the water and noting how much line was payed out when the lead weight reached the bottom. Sailors referred to this as "heaving the lead."

Taking soundings by the old-fashioned method is time-consuming, however, especially in deep water. Today most depth measurements are made using an *echo sounder*. Instead of dropping a weight, a pulse of sound energy is transmitted electronically toward the bottom. The time it takes the pulse to travel to the bottom and be reflected back up to the surface is measured. From this time interval can be calculated the depth of the water. When pulses are sent out and received in quick succession, an almost continuous recording of the ocean depth called a *bottom profile* may be obtained.

When a geological oceanographer examines the rock that makes up a large portion of the continental land mass and compares it to the solid rock that is underneath the ocean floor, he finds that they are very different. Continental rock is primarily composed of granite, while the rock found underneath the oceans is basalt. These two rocks are not only different in appearance, but also in weight and chemical composition. Merely by examining

Above: Continental shelf and slope showing submarine canyons.

Below: One type of modern echo depth sounder. Sonic pulses generated by the device electronically travel down to the ocean floor and are then reflected back to the research ship. Elapsed time is automatically translated into a depth indication.

each, a geological oceanographer is quickly able to distinguish between continental and oceanic rocks.

If the rocks in the region of the continental shelf and the continental slope are examined, they are found to be composed of granite, even though these areas are underneath the ocean. The rocks underneath the ocean do not start to become basaltic until after the continental slope itself is left to landward. Thus it appears that from a geological point of view, the continents do not end abruptly at the coastline but at the base of the continental slope farther out to sea.

The Mid-Ocean
Ridge and Rift

If you took a ship out into the Atlantic, you would find the water becoming deeper very, very slowly. For hundreds of miles the bottom is flat and featureless. Then, suddenly, about halfway across, the echo sounder records a hump on the sea floor. Soon there are more humps, and they have become the size of hills. The ship is now sailing above the *mid-Atlantic ridge.* Near the center of the ridge the hills become still higher and steeper. Great mountains 7,000 feet high rise to within 5,000 feet of the surface.

Between the mountains are deep valleys with flat floors. Right in the very middle of the ridge lies the largest valley of all. It is called the *mid-ocean rift.* Scientists think that the two halves of the ridge are moving apart very, very slowly. The rift is a crack between them. Over the years, the crack fills with sediment, and then new mountains rise in it. The new mountains become part of the ridge and begin to move apart. Then a new rift valley forms.

Mid-ocean ridges are found in all the major oceans of the world. Many of the big ridges are joined by another ridge in the Antarctic Ocean. (You can see this clearly if you look at a map on which ocean depths are marked.) Together they form one huge mountain range about 40,000 miles long.

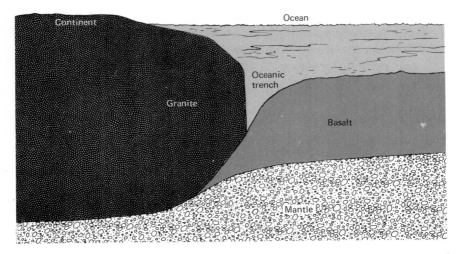

A typical cross section of the earth's crust, showing continental and oceanic rocks.

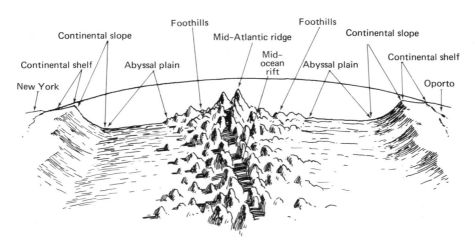

Profile of the ocean floor.

This super-ridge is the longest mountain chain in the world. Usually it rises about 6,000 feet above the sea floor nearby. But in some places the peaks rise above the surface and make islands. The Azores and the Hawaiian Islands are such islands.

Ocean Trenches, Submarine Canyons, and Turbidity Currents

The deepest parts of the ocean, called *ocean trenches*, are found at the geological edge of the continents (that is, at the base of the continental slope). These trenches are very deep gashes in the ocean bottom which run more or less parallel to the coastline at the base of the continental slope. The deepest part of the ocean is located in the Marianas Trench in the South Pacific Ocean at a depth of about 36,200 feet, or almost 7 miles beneath the surface. This is much greater than the depths found in the mid-Pacific basin which range only between 12,000 and 15,000 feet. Thus, strangely enough, the deepest parts of the ocean are found around its edge rather than in its center.

Another type of valley on the ocean bottom is the *submarine canyon*. Submarine canyons usually run across the continental shelf and down the continental slope. In many cases they appear to be the natural extensions of river valleys already existing on the continents.

There have been many attempts to explain the origin of these submarine canyons, but most geological oceanographers today believe that they were probably produced by turbidity currents. A *turbidity current* is a current of very muddy water. There is so much mud held in suspension by this ocean water that it is able to scrape the bottom, much like a piece of sandpaper. In addition, there is some evidence to indicate that these currents travel at extremely

The Peru-Chile trench.

8

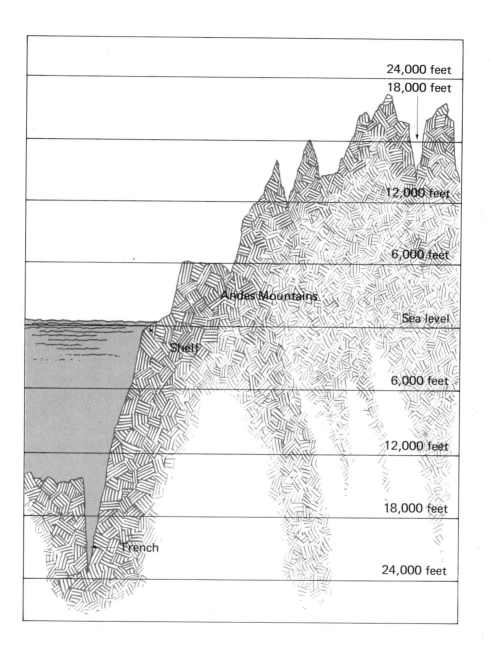

24,000 feet
18,000 feet
12,000 feet
6,000 feet
Andes Mountains
Sea level
Shelf
6,000 feet
12,000 feet
18,000 feet
Trench
24,000 feet

high speeds, perhaps ten times as fast as any other known currents. Such action could well result in a scraping of the ocean bottom, eventually producing deep furrows in the continental shelf and slope.

Sea Mounts

When the ocean basins are examined, the ocean floor is not found to be as flat and monotonous as one might expect. In addition to the canyons, trenches, and oceanic ridges, there are individual mountains on the ocean bottom called *sea mounts*, and even some sea mounts with flat tops called *guyots* or *table mounts*. The formation of an oceanic mountain is an interesting process and was first described by Charles Darwin, who proposed the now-famous Theory of Evolution. Darwin suggested that sea mounts are formed by volcanic action. Over a period of time, a volcano builds up a mound of material on the ocean floor as lava is pushed out of the earth's interior through some opening in the ocean bottom. This lava builds up until an underwater volcano becomes an underwater mountain.

The process may stop or it may continue, with the volcano adding molten lava and building up this underwater mountain so high that it eventually emerges above the surface of the sea. This was actually seen to happen in 1963 in the North Atlantic Ocean, when the island of Surtsey was formed near Iceland. As a matter of fact, all oceanic islands are generally formed in this manner, and they are all composed basically of volcanic rocks that are essentially basaltic in nature.

Over a period of time after such an island is formed, the volcano will eventually become dormant so that the building process is arrested. At this point, atmospheric forces, such as wind and rain, have an opportunity to erode the top of the volcano, tending to level the surface. The molten material needed to form the island came from the earth's interior and left behind an empty space within the earth. Over a period of thousands of years, this cavity will start to collapse and the whole mountain will sink back into the earth from

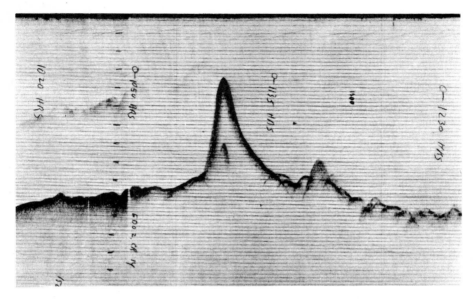

This bottom profile, a chart of the ocean depths made electronically by an echo sounder, shows a sea mount recorded over 3,300 feet high in the Caribbean Sea.

whence it came. Oceanographers therefore assume that whenever a sea mount is found with a flat top, it once had its peak above the sea's surface.

Coral Atolls

Similar to sea-mount formation is a process having to do with coral atolls. *Coral atolls* are small islands that exist in the equatorial Pacific Ocean where the water is quite warm and a tiny sea animal called the coral makes its home. The coral is an animal that develops an exterior skeleton out of hard, rocklike material called calcium carbonate. It lives inside its little house as do thousands of others

11

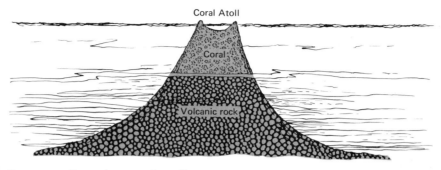

Coral Atoll

Coral

Volcanic rock

Cross section of a coral atoll.

in a coral colony. Usually when people speak of coral, they are talking about the skeletal remains of the animal, not the animal itself.

If a volcanic island is located in an area where coral grows, the coral may very well start growing around the edge of the island. If conditions are right, as the mountain sinks back into the ocean, the coral will grow rapidly enough so that they maintain a layer of coral skeletons above the water's surface. In other words, as the volcanic base of the island sinks back into the ocean bottom, the island itself is still growing on top due to the action of many thousands of these tiny animals. They grow in such a manner that they actually form a new island around the edge of the old one.

Evidence to support this theory was recently obtained at Eniwetok Atoll in the Marshall Islands. Here some geologists drilled down into the coral atoll and pulled up samples of coral skeletons. When they had drilled down slightly more than 4,000 feet, they ran into lava. Here, then, was definite evidence to indicate that at one time this lava surface had been 4,000 feet higher than it is now, for it is known that coral cannot live at depths greater than about 100 feet. Oceanographers are therefore reasonably sure that sea mounts and coral atolls are dynamic features in that they are either moving up toward the water surface or down into the ocean bottom.

Is the Ocean Bottom Moving?

The ocean bottom is very interesting to oceanographers from many points of view. For one thing they find that the sedimentary rocks that exist on the ocean bottom are much younger than any similar rocks they find on the continents. In fact, no deposits on the ocean floor seem to be older than a couple of hundred million years, whereas many rocks on the continents are far older than this. For many years geologists have been asking, "Why aren't there older rocks on the ocean bottom?" and "Where do the older rocks go?"

Furthermore, the mud layers covering the rocks on the bottom of the ocean — the sediments — are continually being deposited, and yet the thickness of this overall layer remains very thin. Again, scientists ask: "Where do these sediments go?" "Why aren't the sediments much thicker on the ocean bottom than we find them to be?"

The answers to these questions have been found in modern measurements which indicate that the ocean bottom must be in motion. It is moving at a speed of from about one-half to six inches a year, and it seems to be doing so in a manner that suggests that the continents also are moving. Apparently the continents can be thought of as floating in a "sea" of basalt (that is, the ocean bottom rocks).

Scientists think that many millions of years ago all the continents were joined together in two huge land masses, called Laurasia and Gondwanaland. Later on in geological time, Laurasia split into North America, Europe, and Asia, while South America, Africa, Antarctica, and Australia were formed from Gondwanaland. But the final picture is apparently not complete, for the sea bottom is still moving and evidently the continents are moving too. Where they will be a few million years from now scientists can only guess.

As far as oceanographers can now tell, the reason for this movement is that the rock beneath the earth's crust (the mantle) is a somewhat fluid substance. It will move in much the same manner as water, but of course much more slowly. With the earth being warmer in the interior, convective currents or vertical heat motions are set up in much the same way that air in a room moves from the floor to the ceiling when an electric heater is placed on the floor. Of course, when the moving mantle material reaches the underside of the crustal rocks (the ocean bottom), it spreads out to the sides. It is this horizontal motion that causes the ocean bottom and the continents to move.

Eventually, the mantle material must return to the interior of the earth, because any such material that comes from there must be replaced. In this manner, the older rocks on the underside of the oceanic crust are dragged down into the earth, which explains why the older rocks cannot be found. Similarly, the older sediments are also carried away as they build up. Measurements have been made that indicate that the rocks very close to the mid-Atlantic ridge in the North Atlantic Ocean have very recently risen from the interior of the earth, while at points farther away from the mid-Atlantic ridge, it was found that the age of the rocks increased. Thus, by noting the rock age measurements and the distance between samples, it is possible for scientists to calculate the rate at which the sea floor is spreading — which works out to be between one-half and six inches per year.

Ocean Sediments
and Abyssal Plains

Covering most of the sea floor is a layer-like blanket of various sediments that is continually being replenished from four different sources. The first of these is composed of the plants and animals that lived and died in the sea. Their skeletal remains or shells form *biological sediment*. This type of sediment is sometimes referred to as *ooze*, which is quite descriptive of its gooey consistency.

The second type of sediment has been termed *erosion sediment*,

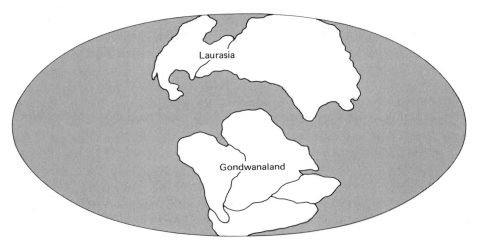

The two primeval continents, Laurasia, consisting of North America, Europe, and Asia; and Gondwanaland, consisting of South America, Africa, Antarctica, and Australia.

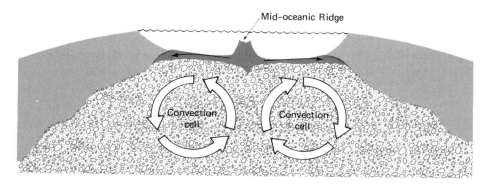

Convection cells in the earth's mantle causing motion of the ocean bottom.

since it results from the erosion of the continents. Silt, clay, and sand are carried down to the ocean by rivers and then transported from the continental shelf area to the ocean basins, usually by turbidity currents. Thus the middle of the ocean has on its bottom material that was once a part of the highest continental land mountains.

This sedimentary material is settling continuously on the ocean bottom in a manner similar to a snowfall. Just as fallen snow smooths out surface irregularities on land, so ocean sediment tends to cover all the rough features of the ocean bottom. Large areas of the ocean basins are therefore relatively smooth due to this sedimentary blanket, and are called *abyssal plains*.

The third type of sediment found on the ocean bottom, although admittedly it does not amount to very much, is *outer space sediment*. Many millions of small meteorites strike the sea surface every year and drift downward to the bottom. These are usually tiny pieces of material that make up a very small percentage of the aggregate on the bottom, but it is nevertheless a measurable amount.

Lastly there are *chemical sediments*. These are materials produced by chemical reactions. For example, in certain areas calcium carbonate will be formed (or, as chemical oceanographers would says, *precipitated*) on the bottom as a result of too much of this material being dissolved in the water. Such formations occur around the Bahama Islands in the Atlantic Ocean and result in extremely white bottom materials.

Another example of a chemical sediment is manganese nodules. These are lumps of rock, some about as big as a man's fist, which cover large portions of the ocean bottom. If one of these rocks is cut in two, it looks very much like the end of a log. There are rings indicating growth, but instead of growing as a tree does, a nodule

Whitish chemical sediments of the type produced in the Bahamas.

grows by adding successive onion-like shells, each individually deposited by chemical action.

These nodules are rather rich in metals such as manganese, tin, and nickel. It is thought that they might eventually be mined. from the ocean floor by a sort of vacuum cleaner device which could suck the material up and deposit it aboard a ship.

Oceanographic Bottom Samplers

The ocean bottom may be inspected by underwater cameras or underwater television sets. However, if a more detailed analysis is desired, a sample of bottom material can be collected by some sort of a sampling device. One such device is the *orange peel sampler*, a clawlike mechanism which obtains a specimen of the upper few inches of the bottom.

A somewhat more common device for sediment entrapment is the coring tube. A *coring tube* is basically a piece of pipe with a heavy weight on the top. This is allowed to embed itself in the ocean bottom under its own weight. It is then lifted up, bringing back to the surface a long, rod-shaped sample of mud representative of the sediment on the bottom. Such a *core*, or *core sample*, shows the different layers of sediment that have been deposited over many years at this particular spot on the ocean floor.

By examining the cores, geological oceanographers can determine a great deal about past oceanic history. Also, the temperature of the water over the last few thousand years may be estimated simply by examining the types of shells of organisms that have been deposited in such sediment. Some organisms will live in warm waters while others will live only in cold waters. Thus the types of organisms found indicate the average temperature of the water at the time the material was formed. Similarly, large amounts of volcanic dust would indicate that some sort of volcanic activity occurred just before the time of deposition.

The Ocean's Saltiness

As everyone knows, there is salt in the ocean. Somewhat less known is the fact that the ocean contains many other substances as well. Just about every known substance is found dissolved in seawater, although many of these elements are present in such small quantities that they cannot be recovered without spending a great deal of money to extract them. For example, small quantities of gold, copper, zinc, iron, uranium, and silver are all dissolved in seawater. Magnesium, on the other hand, is dissolved in such large amounts that it is very profitable to extract it from seawater. In fact, most of the magnesium used in aircraft manufacture is obtained in this manner.

Ten chemical elements make up over 99 percent of the material dissolved in seawater. These are: chlorine, sodium, magnesium, sulfur, calcium, potassium, bromine, carbon, strontium, and boron.

When a chemical oceanographer talks about the saltiness, or *salinity*, of seawater, he is not just talking about the common salt (sodium chloride) present in the ocean, but *all* of the dissolved materials. On the average, the salinity of seawater is such that about $3^{1}/_{2}$ percent of the weight of a sample volume of seawater is dissolved materials, while the rest is water. What are the sources of this salinity?

One source is the continents themselves. Continental rocks and minerals are dissolved by water action and carried down into the ocean by rivers. However, it turns out that this is a relatively small source of the ocean's dissolved materials. In fact, some substances such as iron are found in large quantities in rivers but are not found in the oceans to any great extent. Actually, the major source of oceanic salts is the interior of the earth. But how do these minerals come to be dissolved in seawater?

Scientists believe that when new rock such as granite is being formed, the molten material gives off liquid and other materials when it solidifies. In this way water, sodium, chlorine, magnesium, sulfur, calcium, and many other substances are produced. Such substances are released through hot springs and volcanoes which, when they reach the sea, turn out to be an adequate source for the dissolved materials in the ocean. It has been calculated that if volcanoes and hot springs had been operating at the same rate as they are now for all of geologic history, they would account for one hundred times the amount of salts actually dissolved in the ocean today.

If the salinity of ocean waters is analyzed, it is found to vary only slightly from place to place. Nevertheless, some of these small changes are important. There are three basic processes that cause a change in oceanic salinity. One of these is the subtraction of water from the ocean by means of *evaporation* — conversion of liquid water to water vapor. In this manner, the salinity is increased, since the salts stay behind. If this is carried to the extreme, of course, white crystals of salt would be left behind; this, by the way, is how much of the table salt we use is actually obtained.

The opposite of evaporation is *precipitation*, such as rain, by which water is added to the ocean. Here the ocean is being diluted so that the salinity is decreased. This may occur in areas of high rainfall or in coastal regions where rivers flow into the ocean. Thus salinity may be increased by the subtraction of water by evaporation, or decreased by the addition of fresh water by precipitation or runoff.

Normally, in tropical regions where the sun is very strong, the ocean salinity is somewhat higher than it is in other parts of the world where there is not as much evaporation. Similarly, in coastal regions where rivers dilute the sea, salinity is somewhat lower than in other oceanic areas.

A third process by which salinity may be altered is associated with the formation and melting of sea ice. When seawater is frozen, the dissolved materials are left behind. In this manner, seawater directly beneath freshly formed sea ice has a higher salinity than it

Midshipmen prepare to lower an orange peel sampler.

did before the ice appeared. Of course, when this ice melts, it will tend to decrease the salinity of the surrounding water.

In the Weddell Sea, off Antarctica, the densest water in the oceans is formed as a result of this freezing process which increases the salinity of cold water. This heavy water sinks and is found in the deeper portions of most of the oceans of the world.

How Oceanographers Take Water Samples — Nansen Bottles and Hydrographic Casts

When a chemical oceanographer wants to collect a water sample, he uses a device called a *water bottle.* The most common of these is the *Nansen bottle* which consists of a piece of pipe with a valve at each end. This bottle is fastened to a cable and lowered into the water to the depth at which a sample is desired. By means of a "messenger" — a weight that is able to slide down the cable — the bottle is caused to be turned upside down. When the bottle turns upside down, the valves close and a water sample is collected. This is then hauled up to the surface for examination by the investigator.

Usually a large number of Nansen bottles are placed on the same piece of cable, each at a different location. This is called a *hydrographic cast.* To the bottom of each bottle is attached a messenger which will eventually trip the next lower bottle, and so on all the way down the line. In this fashion, samples may be obtained at many different depths on the same piece of cable at the same time.

One of the main advantages of using Nansen bottles or some similar device is that reversing thermometers may be attached to them. When inverted, reversing thermometers will permanently

A geological oceanographer checks a coring tube, used to obtain rod-shaped samples of sediment from the ocean bottom.

23

HYDROGRAPHIC CAST

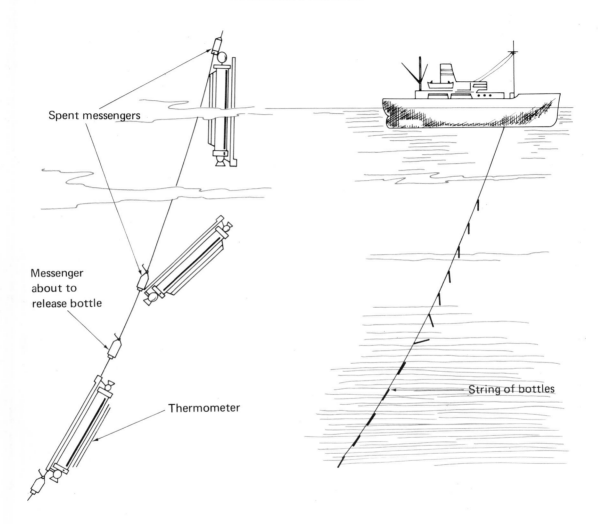

Spent messengers

Messenger about to release bottle

Thermometer

String of bottles

Bottles capture samples of water at various depths. Cast is then pulled on board ship, and salinity of water samples is determined.

(until they are turned right side up) indicate the water temperature present at the moment they were upended. In this way, the ocean scientist is able to read the temperature of the water when it was trapped within the bottle. By using many Nansen bottles, each having a reversing thermometer, a large number of different depth water samples, together with their temperatures, may be obtained simultaneously.

The Ocean's Temperatures

The temperature of the ocean is never the same everywhere. Not only does the water temperature get cooler nearer the poles, but the deeper water is also colder than that near the surface.

Generally speaking, the ocean can be thought of as being made up of two layers: an upper layer that is relatively warm, and a lower layer that is relatively cold. In between these two, there is a layer of change, from warm at the top to cold at the bottom, called the *main thermocline.*

Oceanographers have little doubt that this layering is caused by the sun. The sun, of course, produces by radiation large amounts of heat, and the only place this heat can penetrate the ocean is at its surface. Actually, the sun's rays include ultraviolet radiation, visible light, and infrared radiation (commonly referred to as heat). Only about half of the sun's energy reaching the ocean surface is in the form of light. The other half is mostly heat.

The ocean is able to admit visible light much more readily than ultraviolet or infrared, so that within the top few feet of the sea surface, more than half of the energy received from the sun is absorbed and serves to heat up the ocean. Any swimmer who has ever dived a few feet below the surface has experienced colder water near the bottom. This is simply due to the fact that a large portion of the sun's energy is absorbed by the upper layers of the water.

This heating up of large volumes of ocean water has been

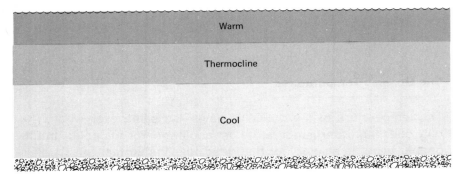

The layer-cake ocean with its warm surface water, cool bottom water, and thermocline in between.

going on for millions of years, resulting in a warm water layer that at various times is as thick as 2,000 feet. However, in most of the ocean it is somewhat thinner than this. Oceanographers normally find that in mid-latitudes the top layer of the ocean is about 1,500 feet thick and has a temperature of about 60 degrees Fahrenheit. The main thermocline (the region where the temperature changes a great deal) is usually about 1,000 to 1,500 feet thick and therefore extends down to a depth between 2,000 and 3,000 feet. Below this, for another 10,000 feet or so, is the deep layer of the ocean which has a temperature somewhere between 35 and 40 degrees Fahrenheit.

The warm mixed layer is somewhat thinner in the tropics, as is the main thermocline. Near both the North and the South poles the deep layer comes right to the surface. There is no warm layer or

Warmer

Seasonal Thermocline

Warm

Thermocline

Cool

The seasonal thermocline found during all seasons except winter in middle latitudes.

thermocline in these regions simply because the sun does not shine strongly enough to heat up the surface layers.

In middle latitudes the temperature structure is somewhat more complicated than this, in part because there is such a large seasonal change in the amount of sunshine received at the ocean's surface. Since these changes take place over a period of only a few months, there is not enough time to heat a very thick layer of water. What happens is that the upper few hundred feet of water do get heated more than the water below during the spring, summer, and fall. This produces a miniature version of the entire ocean within the upper warm layer.

During the summer, for example, there is a thin warmer surface layer having a temperature of perhaps 75 degrees Fahrenheit and a thin seasonal thermocline, both located at the top of the previously described warm layer which has a temperature of about 60 degrees Fahrenheit. For three-quarters of the year then, the middle-latitude ocean contains two thermoclines rather than one.

**The Bathythermograph —
A Thermometer on a String**

In addition to reversing thermometers for measuring temperature, there are two other types utilized by physical oceanographers. These two devices are each a kind of *bathythermograph* (*bathy*-depth, *thermo*-temperature, and *graph*-picture), usually known as BT's. Both present a picture of the variation of temperature with depth.

The first, the mechanical bathythermograph (BT) is lowered by means of a strong wire cable and is retrieved at the end of each observation. The second, the expendable bathythermograph (XBT), falls to the bottom of the sea after an observation and is never recovered.

In the BT a gold-coated glass slide is placed in the unit and used for the graph. This is drawn by a stylus, or scratching point, connected to a temperature-sensitive tube. This tube expands and contracts with changes in temperature, causing the stylus to move as the temperature changes. The carriage holding the slide is attached to a depth-sensitive bellows so that, as the depth of the BT changes, the slide moves. As the device is dropped down into the water, the increasing depth causes the slide to move to the left while the decreasing temperature causes the stylus to move down so that a graph is made of temperature versus depth on the slide.

The XBT is much smaller and easier to use than the mechanical BT, since there is no need to worry about getting it back. The XBT has a little electrical element that sends a temperature signal up a thin wire. The other end of this wire is attached to a large electronic case containing graph paper aboard ship. As the XBT falls through the water, this temperature signal is recorded on a piece of moving

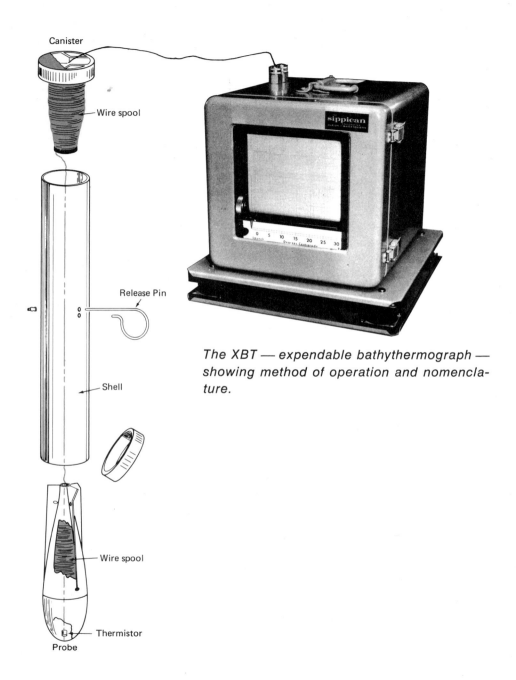

Canister

Wire spool

Release Pin

Shell

Wire spool

Thermistor

Probe

sippican

0   5   10   15   20   25   30

The XBT — expendable bathythermograph — showing method of operation and nomenclature.

graph paper. Since the expendable bathythermograph is designed to fall through the water at a known speed, its depth at any time after it is dropped may easily be determined. In this manner, the XBT also gives a graph of temperature versus depth. However, the graph obtained with the XBT is not a small glass slide but a large piece of paper which is much easier to read.

The mechanical BT is lowered and raised at the end of a cable usually while the ship is moving at a speed between five and ten knots (one knot equals a speed of one nautical mile — 6,080 feet — per hour). The XBT, however, since it is much smaller, may be lowered while traveling at speeds up to 30 knots. The device is simply lowered into the water. When it reaches the end of the wire, the wire breaks, and the unit continues to fall to the bottom. By using these two "thermometers on strings," it is possible for ocean-ographers to determine how temperature changes with depth in the ocean. This is of great interest if the investigator is concerned about where to search for fish or what types of currents are present.

Waves and Their Energy

Waves are bumps and creases on the ocean's surface that tend to repeat themselves. The high spots are called *crests* while the low areas are *troughs*. The horizontal distance between two adjacent crests or two adjacent troughs is the *wavelength*, and the time it takes one wavelength to pass a fixed point is the wave *period*. The wave *height* is the vertical distance from crest to trough.

Waves are one of nature's favorite methods of moving energy from one place to another, and this can be easily seen in the ocean. The wind blows somewhere over the ocean and waves are produced, because some of the energy of the wind is transferred to the sea surface. These waves then start to move, and they carry with them the energy initially given them by the wind. The waves may move for thousands of miles, carrying this energy until they reach some beach or shallow area. There the waves break, expending their energy with thunderous crashes on the shoreline.

Most of the waves we see on the ocean surface are produced by the action of wind. The size of these waves is related to three properties of the wind. These are the speed of the wind, the duration (the total time that the wind blows), and the *fetch* (the distance over which the wind blows). The longer the duration and the fetch for a particular wind speed, the bigger the waves that will be produced. However, this situation does not hold true indefinitely, because the waves for a particular wind speed will grow only up to a certain size and no larger. This condition is called a *fully developed sea.* No matter how much longer the wind blows after this maximum size has been reached, the waves will not get any bigger. Generally speaking, as the wind speed increases, the fully developed sea shows waves having greater wave heights, lengths, and periods.

Wind waves may build up to tremendous heights. In the open ocean, waves as high as 110 feet have been reported. Such huge waves would be as high as a building eleven stories tall. These are frightening natural occurrences, and many ships have been overturned by smaller waves than this. Fortunately, however, waves this high are extremely rare. As a matter of fact, wind-generated waves higher than 30 or 40 feet are very unusual. Since wave height is directly related to the wind speed, high waves would be expected as a result of strong winds such as may be experienced in a hurricane. And, indeed, hurricanes do produce extremely heavy seas and high wind waves. However, the other two properties of fetch and duration must also be considered. Hurricanes typically cover only a few hundred miles in area and therefore contain a relatively small fetch. Even though wind speeds in the hurricane may be 100 knots or more, the waves produced are not as high as they could be due to the fetch limitation. Nevertheless seas produced by a hurricane are extremely dangerous, and experienced seamen know they should be avoided at all costs.

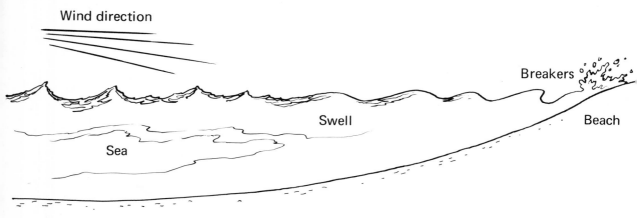

The life history of wind waves as they move from the generating area to the beach.

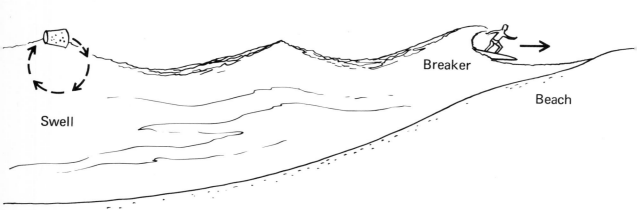

The cork in swell moves back and forth as the waves transport energy, not water. The surfer moves toward the beach as breakers transport energy and water.

Sea, Swell,
and Wave Motion

In a deep ocean region where the wind is blowing and creating waves, the waves are all different sizes and shapes, and they are all going in different directions at the same time. This situation where the waves are irregular in size and shape is termed a *sea*. As the waves move out from this generation area, carrying their energy with them, the longer waves will move faster than the shorter waves, leaving the shorter waves behind. This will tend to separate the waves into groups so that, after a while, instead of having long waves and short waves all together, the waves traveling together are all about the same length. In this condition, the waves are called *swell* because the waves are long and smooth.

If we look closely at a wave, we see an apparent up-and-down motion because there is a moving bump on the surface of the water. If we put a cork in the water and watch its motion as the wave goes by, the cork is seen to move up and down and back and forth in the same place, but it does not move along with the wave. From this we are able to deduce that as the wave goes by, energy is being carried with it, but not water. Thus, waves are a means by which energy can be moved, not water. At a particular spot, of course, a chunk of water is moving first in one direction, then another, but it will always end up in the same place it started after the wave has gone by.

Breaking Waves
and Rip Currents

When the wave gets into relatively shallow water, it is affected by the bottom and tends to travel more slowly. This means that a group of wave crests entering shallow water will tend to pile up because the crests in front are not going as fast as those behind. This piling up will cause the wave heights to increase somewhat, and finally the waves will *break* as the water in the crest simply spills over into the trough of the wave ahead. At this point, the wave ceases to be a "true" wave, since both water and energy are moving toward the beach together.

Once the wave has broken, its energy is gone and the water that moved with the wave has spilled up on the beach and must now return to the ocean. This return of water from breaking waves is usually concentrated at selected places and is called a *rip current*. The location of rip currents along a beach may vary from day to day as the type and source of the swell changes.

Tsunami

Another kind of large wave occasionally seen, especially in the Pacific Ocean, is the so-called "tidal wave." However, since these waves really have nothing to do with the tide, physical oceanographers now call them *tsunami* (the Japanese word for them).

A tsunami is actually a wave caused by an underwater earthquake; hence, it is sometimes referred to as a *seismic sea wave.* Tsunami are hardly noticeable in the open ocean and most of them are quite harmless even when they break on the beach. However, occasionally when they reach shallower water, they develop into tremendous breaking waves as high as 30 or 40 feet. When large waves of this size break on a beach, they will tend to swamp the entire coastal area, causing great damage and serious flooding conditions. Large numbers of lives have been lost in places such as Japan and Hawaii due to tsunami.

Tsunami always produce higher waves in shallow areas than they do in mid-ocean, since the water piles up when coming inshore. While the waves produced by hurricanes primarily endanger ships, tsunami are especially dangerous to shore-based structures.

The Tides

On the eastern coast of Canada, near the entrance to the St. Lawrence River, lies the Bay of Fundy. The water in the Bay of Fundy moves in and out twice a day — but in such a dramatic manner that at certain times the water level is 40 feet higher than it is at other times. This periodic change in water level is one of the most impressive examples of tides in the world. Yet there are a few other places on the globe where tides almost as large are found, one of them being the harbor of Anchorage, Alaska, which has a tidal range of about 35 feet.

In most parts of the world, the rise and fall of water, usually occurring twice a day (two high tides and two low tides every twenty-five hours) amounts to only a few feet. Nevertheless, this change in water level still is enough to be very important in some areas. In many places at low tide, the water is too shallow to allow boats to move effectively into and out of harbors, whereas at high tide it is deep enough for them to do so. Because of their effect on navigation, tides have been studied for many years, and today physical oceanographers know quite a bit about their causes and characteristics.

Tides are really very, very long waves. They are caused by the gravitational attraction of the sun and the moon for the earth and its oceans. Due to the fact that the distance from the moon to the center of the earth is not the same as the distance from the moon to the ocean, a different gravitational force is exerted on the movable water of the oceans than on the earth itself. This difference in gravitational attraction between the water covering the earth and the earth itself is enough to produce a bulge in the ocean. With the moon, for example, on one side of the earth, the moon will attract the water closest to it more than the earth; consequently, this mass of water will be pulled toward the moon. At the same

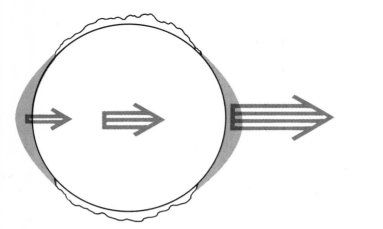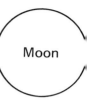

The moon acting on the earth and the oceans to produce two oceanic bulges.

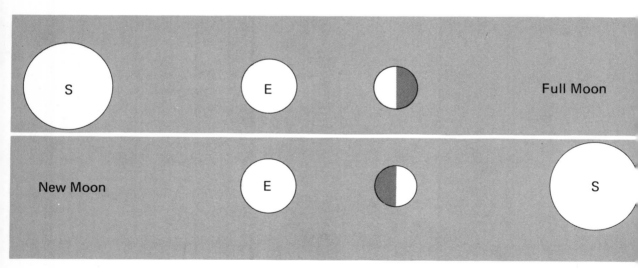

The moon and sun acting together produce spring tides at new moon
and full moon periods. These conditions are termed syzygy and happen every fourteen days.

time, the moon will not attract the water on the other side of the earth as much as it attracts the earth, so that the earth itself is pulled away from this water. In this manner two bulges of water are formed, one on each side of the earth.

As the earth rotates on its axis, the planet takes 24 hours for one complete rotation with respect to the sun. But, since the moon is also revolving around the earth, when the earth returns to the position it had on the previous day, the moon has since moved in the sky. It takes an extra fifty minutes for a point on the earth's surface to catch up with the moon. For this reason, a lunar day takes 24 hours, 50 minutes, while a solar day takes 24 hours.

The force that produces the tides is the gravitational attraction of either the sun or the moon, or both. Since this force is primarily related to the distance of the attracting body to the earth, it turns out that the much-closer moon has a far greater tidal effect than the more-distant sun. For this reason scientists find that most tides on the earth are lunar tides; that is, they occur in response to the moon's gravitational pull and therefore have periods related to a lunar day (24 hours, 50 minutes) rather than a solar day (only 24 hours).

We have seen that there were two bulges produced by the gravitational effect of the moon. If we follow a point on the surface of the earth through one complete rotation of the earth, we see that it passes by both bulges. Therefore, for each complete rotation of the earth there are two high tides (the bulges) and two low tides (the places in between). Since a *tidal period* (the time it takes to complete one high tide and one low tide) is equal to half the time it takes for the earth to rotate, as far as the moon is concerned this amounts to about $12\frac{1}{2}$ hours.

When both the sun and the moon are in a line with the earth, a situation called *syzygy* results, producing *spring tides*. Because the sun and the moon are both pulling together at the same time, the gravitational effect is greatest in the same direction, and the resulting spring high tides are higher than at any other time. This is a rather common occurrence since it happens every 14 days, whenever there is a full or a new moon.

About halfway between the full and the new moon, the first or the last quarter occurs. This takes place when the earth, moon, and sun are at right angles to each other (a situation called *quadrature*). In this case, the gravitational forces of the sun and the moon are not operating in the same direction so that the magnitude of the tides is somewhat decreased. This is called *neap tide* and also occurs every 14 days, or halfway between the spring tides.

Why do some locations have much bigger tides than others when the sun and the moon operate on the oceans as a whole? The answer to this question is rather complicated, but generally speaking it is due to two causes.

In the case of the Bay of Fundy, there is apparently a funneling effect produced by the shape of the bay. As high tide moves up the bay, all the water is squeezed into a smaller and smaller area so that the water level is forced to rise very sharply.

In other places, large tides are produced by what are called *resonance effects*. Here the area where the tide occurs is of such size and depth that the natural period of oscillation for the water enclosed is the same as that for a lunar or solar day, or half day.

To illustrate this situation, imagine a basin nearly filled with water. If this basin is tilted and then put back down again, the water will slosh back and forth; the time for each slosh (the *period*) will be determined by the size of the basin and the depth of the water in it. If the depth is increased, the period changes; or if a smaller or larger basin is used, the period also changes.

Now suppose instead of just picking up one end of the basin and dropping it once, one end of the basin were picked up and dropped periodically at the same rate at which the water wanted to slosh back and forth. If this is done, a condition called *resonance* results as the sloshes become higher and higher in amplitude; it then becomes very easy to spill the water out of the basin. As applied to a large oceanic area, if the natural period is $12\frac{1}{2}$ hours,

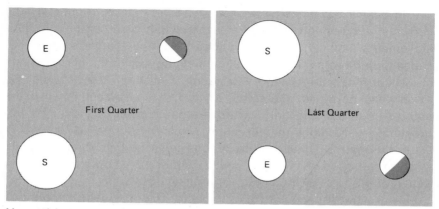

First Quarter

Last Quarter

Neap tides occur every fourteen days when the earth, sun, and moon are in quadrature.

the range in tides (the natural sloshing back and forth produced by the gravitational effect of the moon) would be much greater than if the natural period were different.

Tidal Currents

Associated with the periodic rise and fall, or tide, of the ocean and its tributaries are horizontal water motions called *tidal currents*. These currents exist throughout the ocean and in many bays and estuaries (arms of the sea at the lower ends of rivers) that empty into the ocean. They also exist in lakes but are usually so small that their effects are negligible.

Since tidal currents are associated with a periodic rise and fall of the water, they themselves are periodic. These currents will change their direction every $6\frac{1}{4}$ hours, just as the water level changes every $6\frac{1}{4}$ hours. When the tide current is flowing from the ocean to the shore, this is called a *flood current*; when the water is flowing away from the shore to the ocean this is called an *ebb current*.

In contrast to this simple back-and-forth motion of coastal tidal currents, open ocean currents are somewhat more complex in their movements. Usually, in the open ocean, tidal currents are *rotary* because their direction is continually changing due to the global shape of the earth and its rotation. For example, at noon the flow may be toward the north; at one thirty, toward the northeast; toward the east at three o'clock; and toward the south at six o'clock. By approximately midnight the direction would have veered around to the north again. Just as with the regular tide, the time for a complete cycle of direction changing is usually either $12\frac{1}{2}$ hours or 25 hours, depending upon the location of the observation.

In any event, these currents, whether they be just a simple ebb and flood tide or a rotary type, are periodic and therefore do not flow in the same direction at all times. This is in marked contrast to most ocean currents which do have a constant direction.

Ocean Currents —
"Rivers in the Sea"

In the mid-eighteenth century a young man named Benjamin Franklin was appointed Postmaster General of the American colonies. One of his first jobs was to attempt to improve the speed with which mail traveled back and forth to England. He did this by noting that some sea captains were able to make the trip across the Atlantic much more rapidly than others by taking advantage of certain currents in the ocean. He found that these men were aware of a rather well-developed current in the Atlantic Ocean which came to be called the Gulf Stream.

Franklin made a number of cruises in this area, and eventually published a chart showing the mean location of the Gulf Stream in the Atlantic Ocean. By using Franklin's map, early sea captains

Great Bank of
Newfoundland

Sable Is.

Bay of Fundy

St. George's Bank

Lake
Huron

Lake Ontario

Fort
Detroit

Niagara
Falls

Lake Erie

New
York

New
Hampshire

Massachusetts

Connecticut

Cape Cod

Nantucket Is.

Pennsylvania

Long Is.

Philadelphia

Maryland

New
Jersey

Delaware Bay

Virginia

Chesapeake Bay

North
Carolina

Cape Hatteras

South
Carolina

Bermuda Is.

Port Royal Is.

ATLANTIC

West
Florida

OCEAN

East
Florida

Gulf of Florida

Bahama Is.

A copy of Benjamin Franklin's original chart of the Gulf Stream.

were able to decrease their travel time across the Atlantic. Franklin's was the first known chart of a well-developed ocean current, which may be likened to a "river in the sea."

Wind-Driven Currents — the Gulf Stream

The Gulf Stream is apparently produced, as are most ocean currents, by the action of wind on the water's surface. In the middle North Atlantic area, the prevailing winds are generally from the northeast in the southern portion, and from the southwest in the northern portion. The result of these winds is to cause water motion in more or less the same direction as the winds blow.

Actually the Gulf Stream is not an isolated current but is a part of a very large *gyre*, or circular current system. The Gulf Stream flows northward along the eastern coast of North America, and moves in an easterly direction across the Atlantic Ocean (where it is called the North Atlantic current). It then heads south down the western coast of Europe (where it is called the Canary current), makes a right-hand turn back across the Atlantic to the Caribbean Sea (the Equatorial current), and then flows out into the Atlantic south of Florida (the Florida current). These five currents form a giant circular gyre, and water is transported around and around the Atlantic Ocean in this manner.

Generally speaking, the currents on the western side of the gyre are faster and narrower than those on the eastern side. Speeds of greater than five knots are not unusual near the Florida coast, while speeds of less than half a knot are common off the northwestern coast of Africa.

Of course, there are many other currents all over the world as the accompanying illustration shows. These all exist at the ocean surface and they are what may be called *permanent currents*. They

The major ocean surface currents.

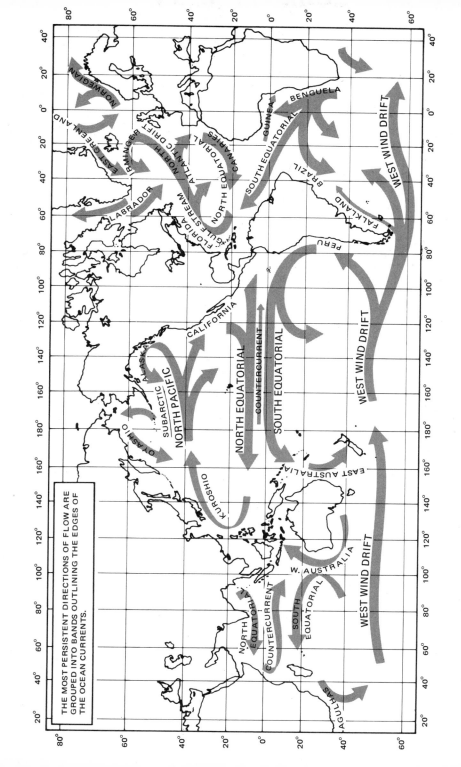

THE MOST PERSISTENT DIRECTIONS OF FLOW ARE GROUPED INTO BANDS OUTLINING THE EDGES OF THE OCEAN CURRENTS.

NORWEGIAN

EAST GREENLAND

IRMINGER

NORTH ATLANTIC DRIFT

LABRADOR

NORTH EQUATORIAL

CANARIES

FLORIDA

GULF STREAM

GUINEA

BENGUELA

SOUTH EQUATORIAL

BRAZIL

FALKLAND

WEST WIND DRIFT

PERU

WEST WIND DRIFT

CALIFORNIA

ALASKA

SUBARCTIC

NORTH PACIFIC

OYASHIO

KUROSHIO

NORTH EQUATORIAL

COUNTERCURRENT

SOUTH EQUATORIAL

EAST AUSTRALIA

W. AUSTRALIA

WEST WIND DRIFT

NORTH EQUATORIAL

COUNTERCURRENT

SOUTH EQUATORIAL

AGULHAS

seem to be present at just about all times of the year with much the same speed of flow.

Ocean Currents
Below the Surface

There are, however, currents in the ocean that exist below the surface. These are just being explored by physical oceanographers, although many have been known to exist for a long time. For example, there are deep ocean currents about 2,000 feet beneath the surface in the equatorial regions of both the Atlantic and Pacific oceans called *equatorial undercurrents.* There is also a deep current below the Gulf Stream, which is found at a depth of about 5,000 feet; it moves from north to south, just opposite to the Gulf Stream itself.

The ocean-current system is thus a very complicated one, although there are only two major causes of water flow in the ocean. As we know, the wind is one of them, and this is by far the greatest cause of all water motion. But there is another fairly important process that occurs when two masses of water having different densities are placed side by side.

Density Currents
and Their Causes

Imagine a tank divided into two compartments. The compartment on the right contains salt water while the one on the left contains fresh water. Due to its saltiness, the salt water is denser than fresh water; it weighs more. When the center dividing panel is removed, the heavier salt water will tend to fill the bottom of the tank while the lighter fresh water will be forced to the top. The heavier water will move to the left underneath the lighter water and the lighter water will move to the right on top of the heavier water. Due to the differ-

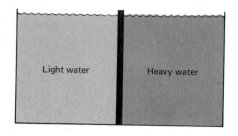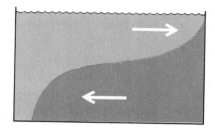

When the separation between the two water masses is removed, currents (horizontal motions) result.

ence in density or weight of the two water masses, there is a tendency for horizontal motion (a current) to be produced.

This variation in density could result from a difference in salt content as in the example above, or it could be produced by a difference in temperature. Warmer water weighs less than colder water. Some parts of the ocean receive different amounts of sunshine than other parts, causing two things to happen. The first is that a temperature difference is produced. The second has to do with evaporation differences. It depends which of these two effects is stronger, since warmer water is less dense than colder water. On the other hand, water having more salt (which would result from evaporation) is denser than water not having as much salt. So the sun shining on a water mass could cause it to be less dense by warming it up, but at the same time it could cause it to be denser by evaporating water and increasing the salinity.

In the tropical oceans, the warming effect is greater so that these waters are made less dense than those in the polar regions. This situation is really an enlarged version of the water tank with two water masses. But the principle is the same, and, due to this unequal water density, there is a tendency for surface waters to drift toward the poles.

A density difference sometimes occurs in smaller regions than the total ocean and for different reasons. For example, when water

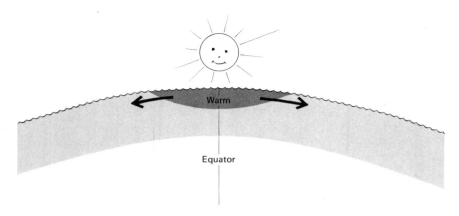

Water near the equator is heated more than water at middle latitudes, causing a surface flow toward the poles.

flows out of a river into the sea, it is causing lighter fresh water to be placed next to heavier salty water. This also results in currents being set up, the cause of which is the difference in water density between river and ocean water.

Oceanographers can measure currents with many different devices. The most common have a small propeller, or rotor, which is caused to rotate at a speed related to the current speed. The faster the current, the faster the propeller spins.

Sometimes water motion is measured by placing a floating object such as a buoy in the water and following it as it moves with the water. Also, sealed bottles or cards that float are often used by oceanographers to measure oceanic flow.

One rather interesting floating device is the *swallow float.* The swallow float (named after Dr. Swallow, a British physical oceanographer) is basically a piece of tubing with a cap at each end to make it watertight. The tubing is so designed that its weight may be adjusted, allowing it to float at any desired depth. When the desired depth is chosen, the swallow float is dropped over the side and allowed to be carried by the currents at the predetermined depth.

46

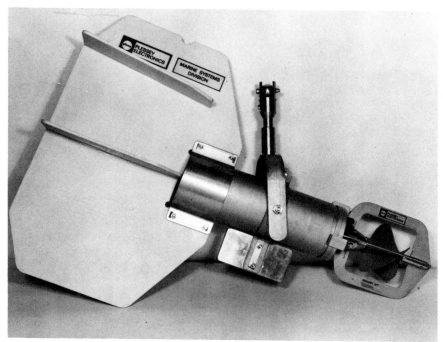

A rotor-type current meter.

By means of underwater sound it is possible to determine the float's position at well-spaced intervals, and thus study currents at any desired depth.

Life in the Sea

Many, many millions of years ago, probably in small isolated pools on the ocean's edge, life began. Somehow certain elements of the primitive slime started to grow and reproduce, and the long evolutionary process had its beginning. Today we find that the ocean is filled with an incredibly large number of life forms. There are big and little ones, long and short ones, multicolored and drab ones, and those that just sit while others never stop swimming. There are even some animals that light up. The simplest way biological ocean-ographers classify the living forms in the ocean is first to separate them into the two primary groups of plants and animals.

Ocean Plants

There are two general types of plants found in the ocean — those having roots that are attached to the ocean bottom, and those not having roots which simply drift about with the water. The rooted plants in the ocean are only found in shallow water. Why? Because their roots cannot reach to the bottom in deeper water and sunlight can-not sustain them. Since plants require sunlight, and sunlight does not penetrate more than a few hundred feet into the ocean, most of the ocean is not capable of supporting rooted plants.

Floating Plants

Nevertheless, plants are found throughout most of the oceanic surface layers. These are the floating or drifting plants known as *phytoplankton.* These wandering vegetables are usually quite small, but they can also be large. Sargassum weed, for example, is a large type of phytoplankton commonly found in the Sargasso Sea. It has stalks many feet long, so that it can very easily be seen with the naked eye.

Although the greatest portion of floating plants consists of very small microscopic types such as diatoms, when large quantities of them are present, they give a color to the sea. Thus, the ocean at times has a greenish cast which is produced by large numbers of phytoplankton. As a matter of fact, the blue color of the sea so com-monly pictured in paintings is the "desert color" of the ocean. That is, whenever one sees ocean water that is azure blue, there is prob-ably little if anything living in such water.

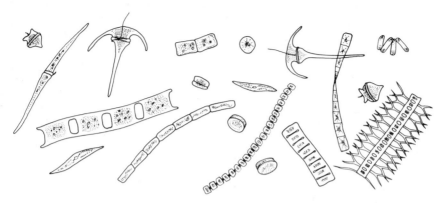

Phytoplankton. These are diatoms and dinoflagellates enlarged about two hundred times.

**Animals of the Sea —
Drifting Animals,
Free Swimmers,
and Bottom Dwellers**

The animals that inhabit the ocean also vary greatly in size. The smallest are the microscopic zooplankton, while the largest are the whales. Some whales are over 100 feet long and are the largest animals that have ever lived on earth. They are even larger than the largest dinosaurs that ruled the earth one hundred million years ago.

Ocean animals may be thought of as falling into three categories: zooplankton, nekton, and benthos. *Zooplankton* are drifting animals and are usually small, but, just as with plants, they may grow to fairly large size. For example, the jellyfish and the Portuguese man-of-war are examples of larger types which are unable to propel themselves effectively and are therefore at the mercy of either wind or current.

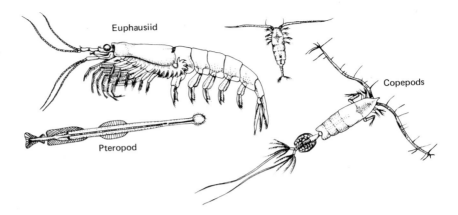

Above: Zooplankton. These are enlarged about fifteen times.

Below: Some examples of free-swimming animals, the nekton.

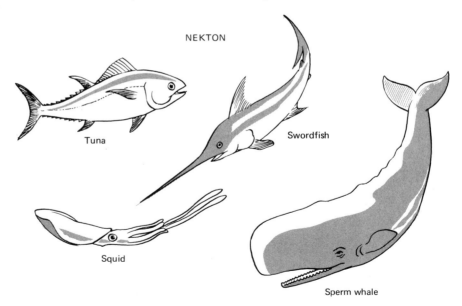

These drifting creatures may be adults or they may be juveniles. Some of the youngsters may outgrow the drifting stage so that the zooplankton are often spoken of in terms of being *permanent* or *temporary*. The permanent forms of zooplankton include the jellyfish mentioned above and also many smaller animals such as the shrimplike copepods which are not able to control their motion with any success.

The zooplankton population also includes some temporary members, such as fish eggs or larval forms of organisms which may grow up and leave the planktonic community to join the nekton or the benthos.

The *nekton* are the free swimmers, and probably the largest portion of familiar animals found in the ocean belong to this class. Common fishes, the octopus, whales, eels, and squid are all examples of nekton.

Of course, the nekton category includes a number of very diverse creatures. The whale, dolphin, and porpoise are certainly very different from codfish or trout because whales represent sea mammals whereas cod are true fishes. Mammals are animals with lungs that suckle their young, while true fishes have gills and lay eggs.

The third type of sea animal spends its entire life on, or in, the bottom. This group of marine animals is called the *benthos*. It includes lobsters, starfish, various worms, snails, oysters, and many more. Some of these creatures, such as lobsters and snails, may be able to move about on the bottom, but their life-style is so bound up with the bottom that they are unable to survive away from this environment. Again we find a diversity of creatures; some are actually able to move about, while others, such as oysters and clams, are fixed in one position for their entire adult lives.

Food Chains in the Ocean

In any particular oceanic area, biological oceanographers can usually find a rather delicately balanced life network. This generally in-

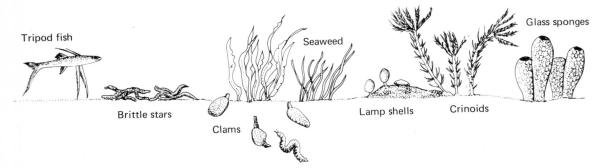

Tripod fish

Brittle stars

Clams

Seaweed

Lamp shells

Crinoids

Glass sponges

The bottom dwellers, the benthos.

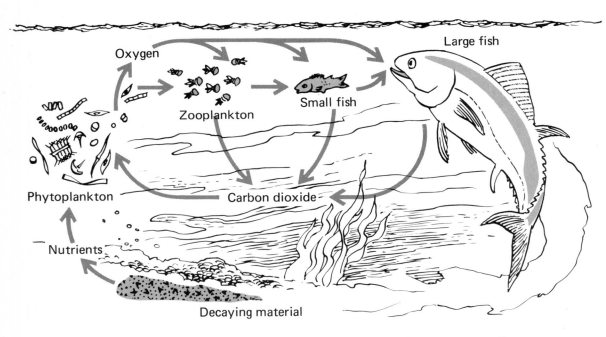

Oxygen

Zooplankton

Small fish

Large fish

Phytoplankton

Carbon dioxide

Nutrients

Decaying material

The marine food chain. Every organism is dependent on every other.

cludes organisms of all sizes living at all depths from the surface to the bottom. These individuals need each other in order to survive. For example, there are many food chains found in the ocean. One food chain consists of zooplankton eating phytoplankton, small animals eating the zooplankton, and larger animals eating the small ones. Man may even take some of the larger animals out of the ocean environment and eat them himself. It has been said that every organism in the ocean is "grazed on" by some other organism. Thus each animal is dependent upon some other life form for his food.

The Deep Scattering Layer (DSL) and Food Chains

A good example of a biological community apparently knit together by a food chain is the deep scattering layer (DSL). It includes animals varying in size from small zooplankton to giant squid, but oceanographers know of its existence mainly because of its sound scattering properties.

Very powerful echo sounders are used to find the bottom in the deep ocean. Oceanographers often notice that their records are spoiled by echoes from quite shallow depths. They know nothing solid is there that could send back an echo. For a time these "ghost echoes" were a mystery. Then it was discovered that the echoes move up and down with the sun. In the daytime the echo is 500 to 1,500 feet down. But as dusk approaches, the echo becomes weaker and spreads upward. At night this *deep scattering layer*, as it is called, is centered near the sea surface. And in the morning it moves down into the depths again.

Evidently the zooplankton have feeding habits such that they migrate to the surface at night and down about one thousand feet during the day. They do not move by themselves, however, since the entire food chain is seen to move as a unit, apparently triggered by the motion of the zooplankton.

Catching Living Specimens

When a biological oceanographer wants to determine the nature of life forms present in an oceanic area, he commonly uses three basic devices to collect specimens. These are the dredge, the trawl, and the net. All three are actually netlike contrivances, but they are designed to capture different sizes and types of organisms when towed behind a vessel. The *dredge* scrapes the bottom, gathering samples of the benthos. The *trawl* is a large net towed through the water to entrap samples of nekton. *Nets*, on the other hand, are made from fine mesh material so that the smaller plankton forms may be collected.

Marine Ecology — the Open Ocean versus Coastal Areas

On land or sea, plants not only provide food for animals but also, in addition, they are involved in the chemical process of photosynthesis, which causes them to give off oxygen and use up carbon dioxide. Since animals require oxygen to breathe and produce carbon dioxide as a waste product, the production of oxygen by plants and their utilization of carbon dioxide is a cooperative venture between both forms of life. *Marine ecology* — the science dealing with the mutual relations between sea organisms and their environment — is based largely on this important balance of plants and animals and how it is affected by the environment. When such a delicate ecological balance is upset — for example, by various pollutants — marine life becomes severely endangered.

Marine plants thrive and grow when there is enough fertilizer (nutrients) in the water and enough sunlight. In the open ocean, the source of nutrients is decaying organic material — that is, dead plants and animals — so that the deep ocean is essentially a closed ecological system. The nutrients — those elements necessary for plant growth — are provided by decaying organisms, many of which once fed on plants during their lifetime. Thus plants and animals live, die, and are interwoven by food chains, and the basic building blocks remain within such a system unhampered by outside influences.

In coastal areas, however, there is an outside source of nutrients, usually supplied by man. This may be fertilizer from rain-washed farmlands, or it may be domestic waste products from city sewer systems. This additional supply of nutrients causes plants to grow much more rapidly than they would if their only supply were decaying organisms. Often certain coastal areas become choked with plant life from this nutrient excess, and this plant overgrowth causes a marked change in the balance between different life forms in the marine area.

This increased growth may be so great and rapid that not only does boating become difficult, but also the entire population of sub-surface creatures may be lost. The plants grow and die so rapidly that all the oxygen in the water is used up in the decaying process of dead plant material; hence there is none left for animals to breathe. This condition is called *eutrophication*, and unfortunately it is found in many of the world's rivers and lakes today.

**Sea Food and
"Farming the Sea"**

At the present time the single most valuable commodity taken from the sea by man is food in the form of fish and shellfish. Man has been fishing the ocean since the dawn of human history, yet in actuality he is still using the same relatively primitive methods of gathering food from the sea as he used thousands of years ago. It is true that he now has larger nets capable of collecting thousands of fish at one time. He also has very sophisticated fish-finding devices using underwater sound techniques. Nevertheless, he is still a cave-

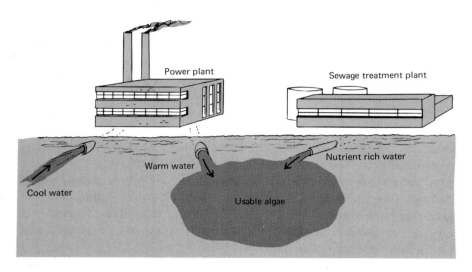

Possible use of two waste products to grow algae for consumption by man or animals.

man at sea. When better ways can be found to study the habits of fish — where they migrate to and why — it will be possible to more effectively utilize the available food in the sea.

One of the first steps that man took on the road to civilization was to grow his own food. Both plants and animals were cultivated and the science of agriculture was born. Yet this has not been done to any great extent in the ocean; man is still a hunter at sea. It appears that until the science of marine agriculture — popularly known as "farming the sea" — is more completely developed, the amount of food extracted from the ocean will remain essentially the same.

Many biological oceanographers have suggested that the various waste products now thrown into the ocean, such as the nutrients mentioned above, might very well be used to our advantage. The nutrients might be employed in fertilizing ocean areas, much as we fertilize ground for the growing of land plants. In this fashion some

Could this sea monster be the arm of a giant squid?

of our pollution problems would be solved at the same time another way of feeding an already overpopulated planet is found.

Sea Monsters —
Are There Such Things?

Reports of sighting sea monsters have plagued mariners for centuries. Almost three thousand years ago an Assyrian king reported seeing one in the Mediterranean Sea. And of course, the leviathan described in the Bible's Book of Job was undoubtedly just such a creature. Yet after all these years, we still do not have a photograph to prove that such monsters even exist, let alone show us what they look like. How, then, do we explain the six hundred or so sightings of sea monsters reported in the last 250 years?

If we disregard the untruths and exaggerations there are two possible explanations for these stories:

(1) They are the result of misidentification of known marine animals. The giant squid, for example, may achieve lengths of up to one hundred feet. This grotesque animal, with two huge eyes and arms perhaps fifty feet long, could frighten anyone, especially at night.

(2) They are the result of sightings of animals as yet unknown to biological oceanographers. There is no reason to believe that every type of animal in the sea has been seen by man. After all, the methods used by scientists to collect sea creatures are really not unlike

a blind man running about waving a butterfly net in the air. How many butterflies will he catch?

Many biological oceanographers are willing to accept these explanations, although there is still a large group that insists on the interpretation that all such sightings have been either hoaxes or honest mistakes. Perhaps as more and more oceanographers explore the sea in underwater craft, the sea monster question will be resolved to everyone's satisfaction.

Oceanographic Platforms
and Submersibles

When an oceanographer wants to find out something about the ocean, he takes his instruments and equipment to sea aboard an oceanographic *platform.* Normally this oceanographic platform is simply a surface ship, but it may also be an airplane, a submarine, or even a satellite.

Oceanographic research vessels have been used for many years. Perhaps the first major use of a ship to gather oceanographic data was from 1872 to 1876 when H.M.S. *Challenger,* a British ship, cruised around the world for four years gathering oceanographic data. Modern-day oceanographic ships such as the *Atlantis II* are capable of accomplishing much more than the *Challenger* because they are able to carry more instruments and the latest oceanographic equipment. While the *Challenger* spent four years at sea gathering data, *Atlantis II* could probably gather the same amount of information in a few months.

In addition to surface vessels, submersibles are also being used in oceanography. A *submersible* is a submarine which is designed for gathering information about the depths of the ocean. Usually a submersible has some sort of glass or plastic window so that scien-

H.M.S. Challenger, *the first vessel to be used principally to gather oceanographic data.*

59

A modern oceanographic ship, Atlantis II.

tists inside can look out and see what the ocean is really like. Interestingly enough, some submersibles are now being manufactured almost completely of glass or plastic so that the entire unit is transparent. The man inside is literally in a fishbowl when he is lowered into the sea.

Unfortunately, the ocean does not transmit light very well, and very little sunlight is present at depths below a few hundred feet. Even with strong underwater lights, it is very difficult to see anything that is more than 50 or 100 feet away.

For this reason, sound energy is utilized a great deal in the ocean for locating objects and sometimes identifying them. Sound energy is transmitted much more easily than light energy in water. Animals such as porpoises and dolphins rely more on a sound system than they do on their eyes. They will make a noise and listen for its echo to bounce back to them from a particular object. From this echo they can determine how far away the object — perhaps a fish — is and in what direction it is located.

Another kind of submersible oceanographic platform is named FLIP (from the words FLoating Instrument Platform). FLIP is very unusual; although actually it is just a very long, thin boat. It is towed out to sea, and, just before it is to be used, the stern of the vessel is filled with water. The stern then sinks so that the entire hull assumes a vertical position. Most of the hull is underneath the surface, but there is a portion that sticks up above the water. FLIP is about 300 feet long so that when the hull is in a submerged working position, scientists can walk down into the waterproof portions of the craft and look out into the depths of the ocean. When the experiments are finished, the water is pumped out of the flooded portion so that FLIP may once again assume a normal position for towing back to shore.

Sometimes oceanographers use a platform that does not move at all. While occasionally large piers are used for studying the ocean, stationary towers are also built in shallow water so that

oceanographers have rigid platforms from which to work. One of this type was built by the U.S. Naval Electronics Laboratory off the coast of California. Many instruments are housed in it which may be lowered over the side as desired. Platforms such as this have the advantage of not bouncing up and down with the waves and remaining very steady in all kinds of weather.

Satellites as
Oceanographic Platforms

The newest kind of oceanographic platform is the satellite. It is not necessary for scientists or astronauts to go along with the instruments into space. Some instruments can be used without human operators, and the data collected is electronically sent back to earth for analysis and study. These instruments may be devices utilizing radar, infrared, or even common photographic techniques. Oceanographers can learn a great deal about the ocean by taking pictures of it, although such techniques are only good for studying the surface layers. Near coastlines, shallow areas may be located and erosion sources may be identified. Very often satellite pictures will show plankton and currents by a difference in color. Polluted areas can also be spotted where the pollutant tends to change the water color.

It is extremely valuable to take pictures of the ocean surface from satellites because a large area is covered in a short period of time. Moreover, it is possible to compare widely separated regions of the ocean for scientific purposes. Such comparisons are not possible with data acquired from surface ships because ships cannot

The U.S. Navy's highly successful FLIP (FLoating Instrument Platform). Vessel is shown here in its vertical working position. Most of FLIP's hull is beneath the surface.

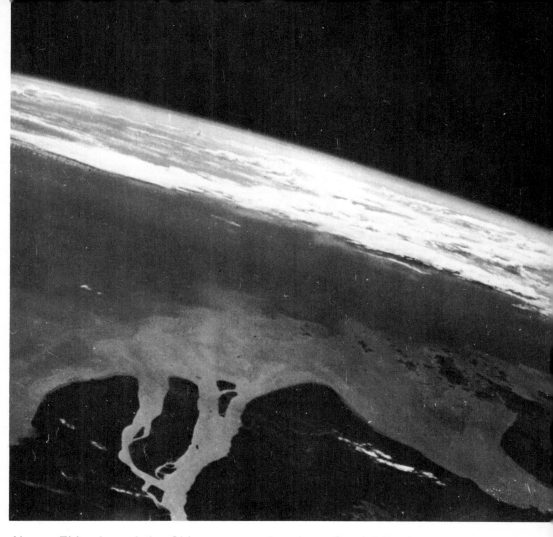

Above: This view of the China coast, taken from Gemini 5, shows silt-mud drifts offshore. Satellites and manned spacecraft are often used to gather oceanographic data.

Left: A stationary oceanographic platform. This U.S. Navy installation is located in the southern Atlantic.

move as rapidly nor can they get so much information within such a short time.

However, oceanographic surface ships are not obsolete by any means. Today oceanographers are using all types of platforms to obtain data, and in this manner as much information as possible is being derived about the ocean.

The Past, Present, and Future of Our Marine Environment

In the past, the world ocean has been treated as being so large that its potential value to mankind — both as a source of food and as a sort of global "wastebasket" — was considered to be unlimited. Fish, whales, seals, and shellfish have been taken from the sea without limit. Garbage of all sorts, from the trash of big cities to obsolete military "nerve gas," has been discarded into its depths. But the world ocean has its limits.

Today environmentalists, as well as ordinary citizens in all walks of life, are beginning to realize that it may be possible actually to destroy the oceanic natural resources if we are not extremely careful in the future. Steps are now being taken to prevent this from happening. Not only are we starting to limit uncontrolled and frivolous dumping into the sea, but we are also attempting to regulate the amount and types of marine life that may be taken from the ocean. New restrictions are being placed on possible polluters, such as drillers of offshore oil wells. Why? Because people are becoming more and more aware of the many things the ocean can offer them and their children.

Two oceanographers conducting research inside a "goldfish bowl" — a small submersible constructed of glass. In the future, larger models of this type will be used.

The lives of many people will be improved in the future as a direct result of intelligent managing of the marine environment. Both marine "farms" and marine "ranches" will become common, as plant and animal crops are cultivated and harvested under controlled conditions. Perhaps even the required fertilizer can be supplied from the waste products of domestic sewage plants, and growing time can be shortened by warming the water with the waste heat from electric power plants. In addition, new methods of extracting some of the now prohibitively expensive minerals dissolved in ocean water are sure to be developed by human necessity and ingenuity.

Even our recreation patterns may be changed as enterprising operators build underwater hotels and campgrounds. Imagine a week spent camping in a "cabin" thirty or forty feet below the surface of the sea. Exciting exploration and collecting in an entirely new world could be just around the corner.

It appears that future exploitation of the ocean is limited only by mankind's knowledge of the sea and his imagination in using that knowledge. Oceanographers will eventually supply this information, but it is going to be up to all of us to determine how best to use it for our maximum benefit.

Glossary

Abyssal plains. Those portions of the ocean floor where all the irregularities are covered with sediment.

Basalt. Rock of the ocean bottom.

Bathythermograph (BT). Instrument for measuring the variation of ocean temperature with depth.

Benthos. The creatures that live on or in the ocean bottom.

Biological oceanography. The branch of oceanography concerned with life in the sea.

Bottom profile. A picture showing ocean bottom irregularities.

Chemical oceanography. That branch of oceanography concerned with the materials dissolved in ocean water.

Continental shelf. The relatively flat, level, and shallow portion of the ocean bottom found closest to shore.

Continental slope. The portion of the ocean bottom next to the continental shelf where the depth increases very rapidly in a seaward direction.

Coral atoll. A tropical island formed by the skeletal remains of coral deposited on a sea mount.

Core. Rod-shaped sample of ocean bottom material taken by a core sampler.

Core sampler. Device used to obtain a core.

Crest. Highest point of a wave.

Current. Horizontal water motion.

Current gyre. Current which takes a circular path.

Current meter. Device for measuring currents; it usually measures both speed and direction of water motion.

Deep scattering layer. Layer of marine organisms that stays within a few thousand feet of the surface and scatters sound.

Density current. Water motion caused by difference in density.

Dredge. A device used to obtain samples of bottom organisms.

Eutrophication. Condition where there is so much plant growth that the dying plants use up oxygen in decay faster than the living plants can produce it.

Expendable bathythermograph (XBT). Device for measuring temperature variation with depth that is discarded after a single use.

Fathom. Distance of six feet. Usually used to specify depths.

Geological oceanography. Branch of oceanography concerned with the ocean bottom.

Gondwanaland. Ancient supercontinent composed of South America, Africa, India, Australia, and Antarctica.

Granite. Primary continental rock type.

Guyot. Flat-topped sea mount. *See Table mount.*

Knot. Speed of one nautical mile (6,080 feet) per hour.

Laurasia. Ancient supercontinent composed of North America, Europe, and Asia.

Lunar tide. Tide primarily affected by the moon, thus having a period of either 12 hours, 25 minutes or 24 hours, 50 minutes.

Messenger. Metal weight used to trigger oceanographic instruments.

Mixed layer. The upper warm layer of the ocean.

Nansen bottle. Water-collecting device.

Neap tide. Minimum range tide occurring every fourteen days during first and last quarter of the moon.

Nekton. Free-swimming animals of the sea.

Net. Device usually towed behind a moving vessel used to collect samples of plankton.

Nodules. Lumps of material found on the ocean bottom formed by chemical processes.

Ocean basins. The major portion of the oceans consisting of all oceanic regions with the exception of continental shelf and slope areas.

Oceanic ridge. Undersea mountain range.

Orange peel sampler. A device for obtaining samples of ocean bottom sediments.

Physical oceanography. That branch of oceanography concerned with currents, waves, heat transfer, tides, etc.

Phytoplankton. Drifting plants.

Reversing thermometer. Thermometer which will not change its reading after being turned upside down.

Rift valley. Undersea valley found in upper portions of some oceanic ridges.

Rip current. Water motion away from a beach caused by breaking waves.

Salinity. The amount of dissolved materials in seawater.

Sea. Sharp, irregular waves found in an area where the wind is blowing.

Sea mount. Underwater mountain.

Solar tide. Tide primarily produced by the sun, thus having a period of either 12 hours or 24 hours.

Sounding. Depth measurement.

Spring tide. Tide having a maximum range; occurs every fourteen days at new and full moon.

Submarine canyons. Valleys in the ocean bottom found on the continental slope and continental shelf directed away from shore.

Swallow float. A device designed to float at any desired depth; used to measure subsurface currents by tracking its motion.

Swell. Relatively long, smooth, and regular waves found at some distance from the generating storm.

Table mount. Flat-topped sea mount. *See Guyot.*

Thermocline. Region of large temperature change.

Tidal currents. Water motion of a periodic nature associated with the tide.

Tides. Periodic rise and fall of the oceans resulting from effect of moon and sun.

Trawl. Device looking like a large net which is manually towed behind a moving vessel to collect nekton specimens.

Trenches. Deep valleys in the ocean floor usually occurring at the base of the continental slope.

Trough. Lowest point of a wave.

Tsunami. Large waves produced by underwater earthquakes.

Turbidity current. A current containing a very large amount of mud in suspension.

Wave. A moving ridge or bump on the water surface.

Wave height. Vertical distance from trough to crest in a wave.

Wave period. The time between two wave crests.

Zooplankton. Drifting marine animals.

Index

Flood current, 39
Flooding, tsunami-caused, 34
Florida Current, 42
Food chain of ocean, 51-53, 54, 55
Food source, ocean as, 55-57, 66, 68
Franklin, Benjamin, 40, 42
Freezing, 20, 23
"Fully developed sea," 31
Fundy, Bay of, tidal range, 35, 38

Geological oceanography, 1, 2-18
"Ghost echoes," 53
Giant squid, 53, 57
Gold, in sea water, 19
Gondwanaland, 13
Granite, 5-6, 19
Gulf Stream, 2, 40-42, 44
Guyots, 10
Gyre, 42

Hawaiian Islands, 8
"Heaving the lead," 5
Hot springs, 20
Hurricane, 31, 34
Hydrographic cast, 23

Ice, 20, 23
Iceland, 10
Iron, in sea water, 19
Islands, oceanic, 10
    coral atolls, 11-12
    as part of mid-oceanic ridge, 8
    of volcanic origin, 10-12

Jellyfish, 49, 51

Knot, unit of speed, 30

Land (see also Continents):
    distribution of, 2

portion of earth covered by, 2
Laurasia, 13
Lava, 10, 12
Lead line soundings, 5
Life in the sea, 47-48. See also Animals; Food chain; Plants
Lobster, 51
Lunar day, 37
Lunar tides, 35-37

Magnesium, in sea water, 19
Main thermocline, 25-26
Mammals, sea, 51
Manganese nodules sediment, 16-18
Manganese resources, 18
Mantle, movement of, 13-14
Mapping of ocean floor, 5
Marianas Trench, 8
Marine agriculture, 56, 68
Marine animals. See Animals
Marine ecology, 54-55
Marine plants. See Plants
Marine ranching, 68
Marshall Islands, 12
Mauny, Matthew Fontaine, 1-2
Melting of sea ice, 20, 23
Metals:
    ocean floor sediment, 18
    in sea water, 19
Meteorites, 16
Mid-Atlantic ridge, 6, 14
Mid-ocean ridges, 6
Mid-ocean rift, 6
Minerals:
    ocean floor sediment, 18
    in sea water, 19, 68
Mining of sea:
    extraction of dissolved minerals, 19, 68
    ocean bottom, 18

Undercurrents, equatorial, 44
Units of measurement:
    fathom, 5
    knot, 30
    nautical mile, 30
Uranium, in sea water, 19
U.S. Naval Electronics Laboratory,
  63

Valleys, ocean floor:
    rift valleys, 6
    submarine canyons, 8-10
    trenches, 8
Volcanic activity, 10, 18, 20
Volcanic islands, 10-12

Waste disposal, in sea, 55, 56-57, 66.
    See also Pollution
Water level, tidal range, 35, 38-39
Water pollution, 54, 55, 57, 63, 66
Water sampling, 23-25
Wave height, 30, 31
    of breakers, 33-34
    maximum, 31
    of tsunami, 34
Wave motion, 33

Wave period, 30
Wavelength, 30
Waves:
    breaking, 33-34
    causes of, 30-31, 34
    crest, 30, 33-34
    defined, 30
    "fully developed sea," 31
    hurricane, 31, 34
    "sea" (irregular), 33
    seismic sea, 34
    "swell," 33
    tidal, 34
    trough, 30, 34
    wind-caused, 30-33
Weddell Sea, high salinity of, 23
Whales, 49, 51, 66
Wind action on ocean surface, 30-
  31, 33, 42, 44
Worms, marine, 51

XBT bathythermograph, 28-30

Zinc, in sea water, 19
Zooplankton, 49-51, 53
    defined, 49

About the Author

Jerome Williams has been teaching oceanography at the U.S. Naval Academy since that subject's introduction by him in 1960 and he is presently Associate Chairman of the Environmental Sciences Department. He did his undergraduate work in physics at the University of Maryland and his graduate work in physical oceanography at the Johns Hopkins University. He has been active in marine-oriented research since 1952 under the sponsorship of private industry, the state of Maryland, and the U.S. Navy. Presently Professor Williams is engaged in projects pertaining to pollution, water clarity, and instrument design. He has published many scientific papers and three books on oceanography. Although this is his first book for young people on marine science, Professor Williams has worked with younger children for many years, helping with the Anne Arundel County public school system's field ecology program since its inception in 1967. He lives in Annapolis with his wife, two children, and various pets ranging in size from goldfish to dogs.